Love's Diary

Lady Stylistique

Copyright © 2014 by Lady Stylistique

Love's Diary

Lady Stylistique

Foreward

Love is a precious gift from God that we all possess in some form and what we do with this gift reflects who we are. As a result, our intimate relationships will either grow or diminish. It's important to understand that love is not determined by what occurs in our relationships. Love is always present but we may not always be present with love.

When I came up with the idea of *Love's Diary*, I decided I wanted to create a poetry book about love as an individual. I wanted to take people out of it and consider love in its purest form. I wanted to explain what happens with love while people experience certain things in their relationships. That's how I came up with the title, *Love's Diary*. If love had a diary of her own, this is what it would sound like.

After each poem, you have the opportunity to write down your own thoughts on love, which makes this *your* personal diary of love.

Inside you'll find beautiful stories that allow you to realize that some of the sayings and beliefs about love are very true in a literal sense. You'll learn the meaning behind phrases such as "falling in love" and "missing you."

There is also the sorrow love has experienced that we feel. You'll discover things such as why it's called "cheating" and what really happens when your heart breaks in love.

These are my own beliefs about how love works. In no way am I saying I'm an expert on love and I am not a psychologist. However, I believe there is meaning in our words and there is a reason why we feel and react to certain things while possessing love as it involves romance. I believe God is always the answer but I also believe that he has created us with love in mind and that we react to love in such a literal way with our mind, body and soul.

Overall, I want you to understand that love is such a beautiful thing and we should appreciate it a lot more. I hope this unique way of thinking about love will inspire you to consider love from a different perspective. So enjoy all of love's secret thoughts as I bring you, *Love's Diary*.

Table Of Contents

If You Come Softly

If you come softly
Life with me is simply heavenly
Waking up in the morning
Is not a burden but a blessing
Because it's more time you'll have with me

If you come softly
Lovemaking is a precious treasure
That life itself could not
Create such pleasure

If you come softly
My heart connects with yours
So your thoughts you'll never have to speak
If you come softly
My hair will be a towel for your feet

If you come softly
The slightest touch warms my soul
A kiss is a taste of a sweet dream
That for a moment is closer than it seems

If you come softly
The sight of my love
Will blind your appetite for women
Whose beauty is disposable, not moldable

If you come softly
Love is a lifetime of bliss
That not even for a moment
Would I want to miss

DIARY

_____

_____

_____

_____

_____

_____

_____

_____

_____

_____

_____

_____

_____

_____

_____

_____

_____

If we realize how precious love is, we would
not play with it and could achieve so much
more than we allow ourselves to. What holds
us back in love is trust. Maybe we've been in
too many relationships where love did not
exist or we have gotten our hearts broken
too many times to possess trust in our new
opportunities.

I don't just mean trusting that your partner
will be faithful. It's also trusting that "what's
mine is yours." Do you share everything in
your relationship? Is it *my* money or *our*
money?

You also have to trust that you are not wasting your time. Are you skeptical about starting a family with someone who could leave you a few years from now?

When you are really ready to let your guard down in the relationship and trust your partner; the love you share with each other is so much more passionate, powerful and beautiful. It's just hard to do when you feel that you can never be certain what decisions your partner will make in your relationship.

Some people say when you know your partner, you start to trust them but we all know people until they do something we never thought they would do. That's why it's called *falling* in love. It's being willing to put everything on the line for the one you love and hoping they will catch you when you fall (I discuss more on "falling in love" in *Love's Value*).

4

Love Is All

Love is all
It is all that is and that need be
To have it and neglect it is better
Than to never know it
Because at least you lived in a moment of all
ALL
Being whole, complete
Full of life and being
A lover or a loved one is a part of all
But it is not all
Because the love of a loved one and a lover
Depends on the love they have for you
They are sharing their love but they are not
Giving you all
The only way to have all is to be all
Give your love to you first
Because nobody will appreciate your love
More than you
But once you possess all, you can be all
So share your love because you can never
Lose your love
When you are all you have
Because love is all

DIARY

_____

_____

_____

_____

_____

_____

_____

_____

_____

_____

_____

_____

_____

_____

_____

In this poem, I attempt to really break down why it's important to love yourself before you can love somebody else. Many of us consider ourselves the most important person in our lives so if we don't love ourselves, we truly cannot love another being. For how can you love someone who is not as significant to you when you don't even love you?

When you love all of yourself, only then can you begin to embark on love because now you know what it means to love and you can share that love with someone else.

Loving someone doesn't always depend on the love they have for you. You see something in the person that has attracted you to them so much that you are willing to give some of the love you have within yourself to them.

Even if they neglect it, don't appreciate it or never return the love, you still have love for them. This is because you are complete by loving yourself.

The Loveseat

I have always been fond of couches
But only the loveseat is where I choose to sit
I have always been in love
So when I sit on the loveseat,
Whether with my lover or not,
I feel special because
My presence on the couch
From the moment I take a seat,
Lets everyone else in the room know that
I am in love
That's why the couch is called a "loveseat"...
Because one who takes a seat
Not only lets the love that burns
Inside of them be known,
They take a seat out of love
Which silently says that
The person is resting...
Resting with their lover...
Meaning that they have found love
And their soul mate
So they are taking a seat on love
And they are never getting back up

DIARY

_____

_____

_____

_____

_____

_____

_____

_____

_____

_____

_____

_____

_____

_____

_____

_____

The "loveseat" personifies what it means to have worked hard in relationships that never worked out. You've gotten your heart broken and have prayed for the one who truly loves you. You may have even had to leave someone that you loved because certain factors in the relationship just weren't worth the hassle anymore.

Then the moment of your life comes when you've found your soul mate and everything you've worked so hard for was worth every tear. Only then will you understand what it means to take a "loveseat."

As this person can finally rest in life and in love. They've lifted a weight off their shoulders and are at peace with their heart. They know they've found the love of their life and they no longer have a reason to get up to search for them or run around in circles dealing with the struggle of dead end relationships.

Chairs & Sex & Sugar

No one comes to sit or play on me
Sometimes I just reside by the table
To make it look good
But when I stand alone
I am a sweet tasteless desire
I thought I was enticing and
Welcoming to everyone
But apparently I am not
I once was pure but someone sat on me
And my unadulterated aura was destroyed
I feel like I get used all the time
People only come when they need to relax
No conversation for the day
Only meant to be mixed with something else
To make it better
Never to be appreciated...as is

DIARY

This is the perfect example of what the outcome could be for not loving yourself first. If you don't love yourself, you have low self-esteem and are gravitating towards whatever gives you a glimpse of love. So you are often fooled into believing you've found love and end up either living in ignorance or hating who you've become.

To be a "sweet tasteless desire" means that people are attracted to you and you are aware of that but when people get to know you or become involved with you, they are disappointed. It's because you don't love yourself and so everything revolves around the opinion of others.

When you leave your decisions in life up to others, you become susceptible to getting used. This is because many people will tell you to do what benefits them, especially if they know you'll do whatever they tell you to do.

Unfortunately, the person that's getting used is not appreciated. But how can you be appreciated if people don't know who you really are?

If you rely on others to make decisions for you, it is time to choose for yourself. Make yourself happy and spend time with yourself to learn what you love. Once you discover yourself, you'll begin to love yourself and people will see that and want to discover you.

Hathor's Love Transformation
As Lioness Sekhmet

Hathor met a beautiful man, Horus
Lord of the sky, sun and war
But because Hathor was in pain
She could only express love
When she was drunk
Although he appreciated her openness
Horus was sad that she, herself
Was not the one saying these things
That it was the wine speaking through her
So he told her to stop
Hathor became angry
And her beautiful face turned fierce
Her hair became a gold mane
Her teeth and nails grew
Long, sharp and deadly
Before his eyes the gentle goddess
Was transformed into a raging lioness
Hathor attacked Horus
And sunk her teeth into him
And drank his sweet, precious blood
When Hathor saw the single, powerful tear

Roll down Horus' face
Hathor believed Horus cherished her
And found joy in that
So she returned to her beautiful self
And because she found joy
In Horus' tear
She was able to express love
And needed to be drunk no more

DIARY

_____

_____

_____

_____

_____

_____

_____

_____

_____

_____

_____

_____

_____

_____

_____

_____

This is my very own story of Hathor and
Horus. If you are familiar with the Egyptian
goddess Hathor, then you know that she
transformed into Sekhmet, known as the Eye
of Ra. She was the overseer for Ra who is an
Egyptian god. When Hathor transformed into
Sekhmet, she became a lioness and was the
goddess of the sun.

As Sekhmet, she went to Earth to kill men
and drink their blood; however, Ra only
wanted to frighten mankind, not kill them. So
he dyed beer red to fool Sekhmet into
drinking it and as a result, she became drunk
and went to sleep.

Hathor had a romantic relationship with Horus so this story is about their love as she transforms into Sekhmet.

The beauty in this story is that Horus loves Hathor and not Sekhmet. Hathor was able to see that being herself is more beautiful and loving to Horus than changing herself to please him. For isn't that what love is about?

True love is not about being with someone who pleases you but being with someone you appreciate. Your desire should be to help this person grow. That's why we share our love with each other in relationships. We are willing to give so that the one we love will become their best.

Cheated in Love

You've stepped out on my love
You've given your love away
You've chosen more
When I am more than what you need
And more is simply more
It doesn't make your soul full
It makes you a fool for thinking more is
More than more
You've infected our love with the impurities
Of what's outside our love
So now I need protection from you
You've neglected love
And the only love I get is what's left over
What you haven't already given away
I'm working hard to maintain the love
We have left
And you walk out on it everyday
I put three steps towards us as you take
Three steps back
You planted a seed in our love
As I thought you wanted it to grow
But it never bloomed because

You never gave it light
A piece of my love died but
I still lived in our love
As you lost sight of it
I've been cheated in love;
Cheated of time
Cheated of peace
Cheated of life...
I've been cheated of love
And I can no longer sit passively
As you allow my heart to break
I've got to seal the love I have left
To give to someone who's worthy inside
And who can put all the broken
Pieces of my heart back together
He'll know that my love is precious
Because my love is once in a lifetime

DIARY

——————————————————————————

——————————————————————————

——————————————————————————

_____

_____

_____

_____

_____

_____

_____

_____

_____

_____

_____

Cheating is the cancer of relationships. It is the reason why so many relationships fail. Whether it's for a year or 14 years, cheating is usually prominent in the relationship's failure. Nowadays, a relationship that has no

record of infidelities is rare, which is very
sad.

For people that don't understand why
cheating is so harmful to their relationship, I
show what cheating means from love's
perspective. Cheating is getting ahead in
your relationship by leaving it behind. You
get ahead by getting involved with someone
else but you leave your relationship behind
by sharing your love with those who are not
your lover.

What is the point of being in a relationship if
you are unfaithful? Why not state what you
want to pursue with someone so that there's
a clear understanding?

Of course people lie so they don't lose their
lover and play games to keep cheating but is
it worth the effort just to keep someone
who you don't value the way you should?
One of the worst things you can do to
someone who truly loves you is to lie to
their heart.

Beauty

Beauty is when someone is pleasured
By the purity of your soul
That shines from the inside out
To be full of beauty is simply beautiful
For it means that your soul of beauty is far
more visible than your exterior
Your beauty delights the senses of another
It becomes influential on their soul
Beauty is powerful
A beautiful soul has a scent, sight, taste,
Touch and sound
Many fall in love with the beauty
Of one's soul
But few love one's soul
This is where the power lies
It can be difficult to see the difference
Just as beauty and pretty are vastly different
To be pretty, one is pleasing and attractive
In a graceful manner
One's soul can be pretty

Pretty is pleasing
While beauty results in pleasure
Pretty attracts one's soul
While beauty influence's one's soul
The love of beauty
Makes sacrifices for pleasure
The love of one's soul drops
Everything to fall in love
The love of beauty sympathizes when
Beauty sings the blues
The love of one's soul can feel the pain
As souls have become one
To love beautiful is to appreciate the
Experience of pleasure from beauty
To love a beautiful soul is to appreciate the
Existence of a soul full of beauty

DIARY

_____

_____

_____

_____

_____

_____

_____

_____

_____

_____

_____

_____

_____

_____

Beautiful means having qualities that delight the senses. While physical beauty is often easily recognized, it's inner beauty that makes us beautiful. It's physical beauty that inspires love but it's inner beauty, the beauty of your soul that makes one fall in love.

Beauty is one of the things that allows us to confuse lust and temporary love with lasting love. Because beauty is so powerful and we may not have ever experienced true love, we will often fall for lust or temporary love, thinking its lasting love. I've given great comparisons on the differences and you really have to take a moment to step away and think while you're in the relationship to figure out the kind of love you're in.

The pleasures we receive physically, mentally and within our soul make it challenging to be logical in love. When you feel excited, loved and happy; you are willing to overlook the obvious because you don't want to lose what you're feeling.

Beauty can seem evil for being enticing but it's simply precious and beauty should be taken in the hands of someone who will appreciate it. If we are not mature and loving, we will use beauty for evil or we may just not be ready to love a beautiful soul.

A Moment of Love

I just needed to stop thinking
Overcome my fear and savor the moment
I didn't care if this
Wasn't leading somewhere
I didn't care what people
I didn't know thought
I didn't care if I was doing it right
I just didn't care because if I did
I wouldn't have enjoyed this moment
This moment gave me life that
I lost many years ago
This moment silenced
The thoughts that never
Led to the love I needed to receive
I may not have fallen in love but I felt love
It is better to feel love than to
Never be loved
Or to fall in love with a lost soul
Because a lost soul doesn't know
What to do with love

It is simply lost
You've wasted your love…

It was a moment of love
My spirit connected with yours
And overpowered my physical body
Influencing me to do things I would never
Think I would allow or do
I spoke with my feelings
And you warmed my spirit
A loving touch filled the hole in my heart
A moment of love has awakened
My spirit to love

DIARY

_____

_____

_____

_____

_____

_____

_____

_____

_____

_____

_____

_____

_____

_____

_____

_____

Sometimes it's best to just enjoy life. We can work so hard in relationships by stressing over situations and possible outcomes. But even after all of that, we could still end up unhappy with love.

We are all at different stages in our lives and some of us will be happier by not being in a serious relationship but for whatever you want to accomplish with love, it is important to take a moment to breathe. This is especially for the person that is constantly upholding his or her standards and wants to pursue a great relationship. This person does a lot of work and should take moments of rest to enjoy a moment of love.

Your standards should be about you and not about what other people expect from you. So if you're tired of being hurt or simply want to have a good time, you should choose to have a moment of love. You never know when you'll want to do that again and not regret it. In fact, it could lead to true love, ironically.

Life is too short to waste your time with people who don't love you but it is also too short to let moments of love pass you by if it leaves you feeling happy.

Heartbreak

My heart breaks every time
I put it in your hands
One of the most precious parts of me
You toss in your hand because
It possesses no value to you
But my heart holds all the love I'll ever have
It is what keeps me alive
Each bruise, tear and shatter
Makes it harder for me to breathe
As my heart experiences a severe burn
That arises in my chest
I have to press the broken pieces together
In hopes that enough love still exists
To mold it back whole
For if not, my heart attacks in defense
To stay alive
But your hands are stronger than
My selfless heart that has lost its love
So you break my heart into tiny pieces

Only to tape them back together
Because you know this confuses my heart
In its tiny pieces, my love is incomplete
It's missing valuable information
That it uses to give my love securely
So you control my love instead of my heart
As I can no longer listen to it
This is the game you play
But my heart, my love, nor is my life
Something to be played with
I should be cherished
My heart is a precious gift
That should only be given to the one who
Places mine in there's
Because a heart survives on love
So the one who does this is trusting
That the love I have in my heart
Will not destroy theirs

DIARY

_____

_____

_____

_____

_____

_____

_____

_____

_____

_____

_____

_____

_____

_____

Breaking someone's heart is painful but to play with a broken heart is simply evil. Someone who plays with a broken heart does not know love. He or she possesses a selfish heart and finds pleasure in heartbreak. Heartbreak is the continuous breaking of one's heart. It causes so much more pain than heartbreaking.

Heartbreaking is the process of a broken heart, while heartbreak repeats this process. The heart experiences heart burn as it makes it hard for us to breathe easily. We touch our heart when this happens to give it some love from our warm touch in hopes it will revive itself. If this doesn't work, studies show that we could experience a heart attack. For those that live with their heart, they could die with their broken heart literally and/or mentally.

Only a strong person can survive with heartbreak and it takes an even stronger person to overcome a relationship where she or he is experiencing heartbreak. One who does will recognize true love easier and will be careful when giving his or her precious heart to someone.

Snow White

Beauty is purer than snow's white
Sadness is darker than the night
Heart is more passionate than love's red
She's given love in exchange for
Blood to shed
Pleasure for prince, pain for her
She sacrifices for him in ways
He'll never know
As he is dissatisfied with the gift she's given
He thinks he's a fool for her trickery
But he can't neglect the beauty
He sees in her
It's a struggle for both
Yet he is not as strong as she
So he uses his fruit of passion as
Poison for her
It's hard for her to breathe
She screams silent
As he grins in charm

But in the moment of darkness
He sees her beauty
And can't sacrifice her soul

To save his misery
She rests in the sleeping death
As she runs away lost in the world
Only to awaken in a fearful ever after

DIARY

_____

_____

_____

_____

_____

_____

_____

_____

_____

_____

_____

_____

_____

_____

_____

_____

This is the story of Snow White with the evil factor being the prince. However, the underlying theme is rape. Snow White is experiencing a moment when her prince does not believe she is a virgin and feels like she's holding back in the relationship so he rapes her, not knowing he is killing her softly. He later realizes she is not playing with him. He discovers her true beauty and finds himself devoted to her.

This annoys him and he believes his only way out of the relationship is to kill her through rape but because she's so beautiful he cannot bring himself to do it.

Snow White finds light in the darkness as she sleeps peacefully through this disaster but she later awakens to see the evil within her prince.

When a woman loses her virginity, I believe the moment should be very precious because it is truly a sacrifice for her. This is why I believe it is taken very seriously for the female and not the male. Men do not endure pain when they lose their virginity. They simply gain a new memorable experience.

A woman has to trust that the man she gives this precious gift to will handle her with care and will not hurt her, let alone kill her. She is literally sacrificing her life to give him a precious gift of pleasure. Would you do that for just anybody or would it be someone that you would be willing to die for? For that is what you are basically doing.

Love's Value

Love is a gift that should be kept
Closest to the heart
It gives you a life of love in a world of hate
For a moment everything seems angelic
You are the happiest you've ever been
In your love life
But your world of hate strains your love life
It could end your life of love or
Make it stronger
A life full of love is more powerful than any
Hate that lies before it
Making love is a temporary way to release
The hate that has disrupted
One with an incomplete life will use
Lovemaking to disguise itself as full
But when your life is love and love is life
You live in love and hate doesn't exist
It seems you've changed but
You've become you...
The being you always were
If hate never existed
You've fallen as a sacrifice in hopes that
The one you love would do the same

So you either fall in love or out of love
But the fact that you were willing to fall
Is more valuable
Than never having the choice
Because if you've chosen to fall for
someone instead of standing for life
Then your sacrifice to live in love is more
valuable than life itself

DIARY

_____

_____

_____

_____

_____

_____

_____

_____

_____

_____

_____

_____

_____

_____

_____

_____

The possession of love should not be taken lightly. When people ask you how's your love life, what they really mean is how's your life of love. They are subconsciously aware that it is a separate part of life. If the world wasn't so selfish or if people decided that love is their life, then life would coincide with moments in love.

People who do not know love believe it is some magical thing that happens between two people that causes them to become so happy that they change for each other.

I believe this is incorrect. In my mind, you develop yourself, just as you do with anything else that is new to you. People change when they grow but they stay true to themselves in love.

Just because someone has fallen in love does not mean they will last in love and that is the struggle people have with trusting the person they've fallen for. When you literally fall down, do you know what to expect?

Yes, you assume you will hit the ground and hurt yourself but you don't know exactly where you'll land, when you'll stop or if someone will surprisingly catch you.

That's the risk you take with falling in love. You'll never know what will happen. All you know is you love this person and you will do anything for them to make them happy or to simply be with them. Even though you don't know if they will reciprocate, you'd still fall for them because the love you possess for them is worth more than the life you've lived without them.

Frostbitten Heart

My heart has been crushed in love
But my soul possesses the love
God has given
So I live with a frozen heart
It's cold and beats for no one
The slightest touch will bring frostbite
My heart has no love to give and
No love to keep
It's been bitten by frost so many times
That it froze
It's protecting and harming itself
Preserving itself for a love so passionate
Is warm enough to melt it
But a heart without a beat is not alive
It is either still or moving against love
It is a heartbreaker
It bites the love inside one's heart
Because the temporary taste of love is what
Keeps its existence
It is manipulative, dishonest and
Not to be trusted

And although it feels powerful in its
Moments of destruction
Nothing fills the hole that was left inside it

DIARY

———————————————————————

———————————————————————

———————————————————————

———————————————————————

———————————————————————

———————————————————————

———————————————————————

———————————————————————

———————————————————————

———————————————————————

———————————————————————

_____

_____

_____

_____

Sometimes when our hearts are broken, we change for the worse. We become the heartbreaker because that's the only kind of love we've been given. Our hope for love is lost and we no longer seek it. If it is given to us, we kill the love because it only reminds us of all the love we've lost.

Some may even thrive on breaking others' hearts. It's the revenge they've always wanted. They feel they don't deserve this pain so they make others endure it so that life is fair in their eyes. That's why it's called sweet revenge. It tastes good at first but it only lasts in the moment because you later realize that it's not good for you.

That's the ironic thing about revenge. You get the satisfaction for a moment and then it sometimes hurts you more than the other person. You know what they're going through and it only reminds you of the pain you've experienced. The victim feels it once, while the heartbreaker feels it twice.

But if you love all of yourself then you always possess love. There are people that love others more than they love themselves. They are the true givers and are susceptible to a frostbitten heart. They survive because even if nobody loves them, God does.

Missing You

The loss of your presence is heartbreaking
My heart recognizes you have left it behind
I know you're coming right back
But your heart is too far from mine
For it to know that

When your presence is near
My heart is complete
As it's connected with yours
But every time you leave
My heart misses you
For when you leave
Our connection is broken
So my heart is feeling incomplete
It's missing you...
It's missing your heart
To be whole once again
My heart beats in search of you
As your heart will play the same tune
So I wear your t-shirts
Look at your pictures
Think of my best memories of you
So my heart will recognize
Your presence once again
As a temporary relief
To re-live your presence
Until you return
I get a natural high from the love
Our hearts share
So no matter the time I spend with you
I am missing you as soon as you leave

DIARY

In the beginning stages of love, we want to spend every moment with that person. Our hearts get so excited about this new love we've found and just want to be close to it.

When we are not near our lover, our hearts think the love is gone because his or her heart is far away from ours. We feel complete with our lover and we miss him or her as soon as they walk away. Their heart is missing from ours to be complete.

We manage through this stage because our hearts realize their love is present, just missing for the moment. That's why we like to keep things that remind us of him or her. It tells our hearts that the love is still present.

There's nothing like those blissful moments of love. For in those moments life seems so easy and you find yourself not having a care for anything else in the world but being with that person.

Cupid's Gift of Love

He pierced my heart
To ignite the love it has inside
My eyes can see the beauty of love
And I could never neglect it no matter
How hard I've tried
My heart beats fast as it finally
Has a reason to live
My hands have a touch of warmth
Because they finally have a reason to give
I listen with my heart
As my ears finally have
A sweet sound to hear
I breathe through my nose
As the lovely scent of passion is finally clear
My tongue dances with yours
As my buds finally agree on what they taste
My feet run to the beat of your heart
As they finally see the need
To keep up the pace

DIARY

_____

_____

_____

_____

_____

_____

_____

_____

_____

_____

_____

_____

_____

_____

Whether it is Cupid's doing or not, when we fall in love we suddenly have the urge to do things we'd never do. We are seeing life in a better view and are inspired to do anything to stay in the present moment because we never know if and when it will change.

When you learn more about the person, sacrifices arise. You may find yourself leaving love behind because it seems like it's not worth the struggle. But then you remember how much you love that person and miss the beautiful moments you shared. So you find yourself consistently drawn to the love you have for that person.

You're living life in a whole new way. It's more powerful and rewarding to you than anything else you've ever done in life. To choose between the best day in life without love and the worst day of love, love will always win (if it's a lasting love).

Sweet Dreams

Now I lay me down to sleep
To rest my mind and for my soul to speak
It speaks to you with love from my heart
So I dream of life with you and
Hope it never falls a part
I sleep in rest, dreaming of you
Because your love is pure and true
Because life is sweeter with you
You are the dream I've always prayed for
And now that you're here, you're all I live for
So I live in a dream and sleep to dream
Because I have a love that no one's seen
Sometimes I need to dream just to believe
That reality is exactly what it seems
And if you're gone before I wake
I'd still give my love for you to take

DIARY

_____

_____

_____

_____

_____

_____

_____

_____

_____

_____

_____

_____

_____

_____

When your reality is better than your dreams, you always feel like you're sleeping. Being with the love of your dreams makes you feel like heaven has entered your heart. It is one of the sweetest gifts to have in life.

Now you don't have to sleep with this amazing dream only to wake up and realize none of it was real. You'll never want to fall asleep and even if you do it won't matter because you'll be dreaming about the reality of your new life.

Of course nothing is perfect but after you've learned that and are able to see the good instead of analyzing the bad, your values will change. Only then will you visualize the love of your dreams and will be that much closer to obtaining it.

Because you've grown in life and love, you'll appreciate the great gift you've been given. So if at some point the love of your dreams fades away, you'll still love him or her because you see that love is not about what you get out of it. It's about giving to a beautiful soul because your hearts have connected and your joy comes from theirs.

Final Thoughts

I hope after reading *Love's Diary* you've grown in love and life. Everyone has different experiences with love and we have to understand that no one is ever ahead in life, especially when it comes to love. Life is not a race; it's a journey.

If you're single now, it doesn't mean you're never going to find someone to love and it's never too late because love never is. Everything will happen exactly when it's supposed to. Not a minute earlier, not a minute later.

Maybe you're in a relationship and things aren't working out exactly the way you hoped. Are you willing to work in your relationship or are you only in it for the happy times? It's also important not to be in a relationship just because you want to be in one. If you're simply just not feeling loved, it's time to go. Love, trust and communication are what I believe to be the most important things for a lasting relationship. However, the most important of these is love. You won't know if you possess these three things without enduring some pain in the relationship and you will usually only tolerate it if you possess love.

I would love it if after reading this book you've found gratification in realizing that you've found the love of your life. Even if you haven't, it is just as great in knowing how to recognize this person when you see them. You've just saved yourself some time and heartache.

If there's one thing I hope you received after reading *Love's Diary,* is to love yourself first. As I stated earlier, if you don't love yourself, how can you possibly love someone else? Besides God, you are sometimes all you have until you find your soul's mate.

Love lives inside you and the more you appreciate the love you possess, the easier it will be to find the one person to give your love to. This is because you've grown to appreciate your love and so you'll be skeptical about whom you share it with and will know when the sacrifice is worth it. So if you've learned nothing else, love *all* of yourself first and everything else will fall into place. Love is a beautiful journey and this has been her diary.

About Lady Stylistique

Lady Stylistique writes poetry out of passion and in order to maintain a peaceful mind. She wrote her first poem at age 13 to mend a friendship. After receiving so much positive feedback, Lady started writing poetry on a daily basis. However, she later realized that poetry should be effortless and inspired, not forced. So Lady decided that it's best to only write when inspired to do so.

After attending a poetry class in college, she gained a deeper understanding of poetry and learned how to grow in her poetry aesthetic. Lady began to write poetry that challenged her skill by writing raw poems that came straight from her thoughts. This allowed her poetry to develop into something that is powerful, meaningful and inspiring.

Lady Stylistique was born from a blog that enriches women on style, inner beauty and confidence. Her brand now incorporates poetry.

Although *Love's Diary* caters to women, her poetry is evolving to inspire everyone. Lady believes her poetry is good for the heart and soul and does not want to deprive anyone from that. So look forward to reading many more works from Lady Stylistique.

CPSIA information can be obtained
at www.ICGtesting.com
Printed in the USA
BVHW040248250920
589621BV00021B/604